Genre Science Fiction

I0799120

Essential Question

Why is taking a break important?

Chill Out

BY PETER FRIEND
ILLUSTRATED BY SCOTT PEARSON

CHAPTER 1

Turbulence

Kris ran past Pedro and Darrel and kicked the soccer ball toward the goal. As he kicked, the lights flickered and the **artificial** gravity disappeared. Without the fake gravity, Kris's feet left the ground, and he felt as if he were floating **unfettered** in space. Kris loved feeling so free, but it was still a little scary. Then the lights went out completely.

"Don't worry," Kris's older brother, Nelson, said, sounding superior as usual. "The *Galactic Princess* is one of the safest spaceships in the universe."

"You shouldn't believe everything you read in tourist brochures," Darrel said.

The lights flickered back on before Nelson could respond. Gravity returned, and the boys slowly floated down to the floor.

An announcement came from a computer on the wall. "The *Galactic Princess* has hit turbulence and suffered hyperspace engine damage," it said. "We must land on the nearest planet for repairs."

Kris grabbed the ball and motioned for Nelson to follow him. Their mom was probably panicking, and she'd want to know that they were okay.

As it turned out, Mom wasn't worried—at least not about them.

"If we don't get to Pentabura tomorrow, we're going to miss our luxury cruise around the Floating Seas!" she said, jabbing at the computer screen. "The little planet we're landing on is dreadful. It was colonized only 20 years ago and doesn't even have one fancy hotel."

Next morning, the computer announced: "The *Galactic Princess* is about to land on planet Droth. It will take three days to repair the ship. You may stay on the ship or take a shuttle down to the charming city of Drothtown."

"That planet doesn't even have a shopping mall," Mom said. "I'm staying here."

"Can I please go down to Droth with Pedro and Darrel?" Kris asked in his nicest voice. "The computer says it's perfectly safe, and our locator beacons and phones will work fine."

"All right, but take Nelson with you," Mom said.

Kris didn't want to spend the next three days with his brother, but it was better than staying on the ship. The four boys boarded the shuttle.

STOP AND CHECK

Why are Kris and his mother and brother on the spaceship?

CHAPTER 2
Unallocated

The shuttle landed in a port full of freight containers. People rushed past in all directions, barely looking at the kids.

"Maybe they don't like visitors," Darrel said glumly.

A man pushing a handcart hurried past them. "Visitors are always welcome," he said over his shoulder. "Just go that way into Drothtown and look for the Allocation Office." He pointed to the right and then disappeared around a corner.

The boys walked in the direction the man had pointed, and they found a large group of people unloading crates from tall six-legged vehicles. Kris couldn't believe how fast they worked.

"Is there a bus that goes to Drothtown?" Kris asked a girl who looked around his age.

"I can take you there," she said, as she quickly unloaded the last crate and climbed into the vehicle. "My name is Yolanda. Now hurry up; you're wasting time."

DROTH
BEETLE 201

Yolanda sat in the driver's seat, and the four Earth kids sat behind her in the empty freight tray. The vehicle moved like a metal six-legged elephant. Nelson looked a bit sick from all the swaying, but Kris enjoyed the ride. He asked Yolanda what people did for fun in Drothtown.

"What do you mean?" Yolanda asked in a puzzled voice.

"What do people do for **recreation**?" Kris asked, trying to hide his surprise. "What do you do after school and on weekends and vacations?"

"I work after school, of course," Yolanda said. "What in space are weekends and vacations?"

Kris thought Droth must be a horrible place to live. He explained weekends and vacations to Yolanda, but she obviously didn't believe him.

"Idleness is irrational. My dad has told me that a million times, and he's our colony commander," Yolanda said **indignantly**. Kris wasn't sure what she meant, but she was clearly annoyed.

STOP AND CHECK

Why does Kris think Droth must be a horrible place to live?

"What a strange girl," Kris said after Yolanda dropped them off at the Allocation Office. He led the way into the building, hoping it was a tourist information center. There had to be something fun to do on Droth. Maybe Yolanda was too serious or her dad was really strict with her.

The man behind the counter smiled as the four boys walked up. He welcomed them to Droth and asked about their skills and experience.

"We're really good at skiing, scuba diving, rock climbing, and playing soccer," Kris told him.

The man frowned and said that none of their skills sounded very useful. "I'll put you on beetle rigging because you don't need any experience for that," he said.

He gave them directions and pushed them out the door, mumbling that he had to get back to work. Kris shook his head and followed his friends down the street.

They arrived at a big blue building, which was full of busy people and more six-legged vehicles. "Those vehicles must be called beetles," Kris said. "We've been assigned jobs loading the beetles."

Then he saw Yolanda and smiled at her, but Pedro, Darrel, and Nelson were **griping** about their new job.

"You're doing useful work, so don't complain," Yolanda snapped. "Idleness is irrational."

"I like being lazy on vacation," Darrel argued.

"Come on, guys," Kris said. "It won't kill us to do something useful for a change."

They all started loading boxes.

STOP AND CHECK

What does Darrel think about working while he is on vacation?

CHAPTER 3
Beetling Along

Yolanda's supervisor had seen her talking to the four boys and assigned her to work with them. They worked hard because they didn't want this strange, unfriendly girl to do better than them.

They finished loading the boxes and climbed onto the beetle. Yolanda said they had done well and handed them lunch without further **reprimands**. Kris was glad—he was tired of being scolded.

Kris bravely tried the odd-looking food and was surprised that it was delicious. He hadn't expected to eat while riding the beetle, but Yolanda said they had to get their cargo to a town called Fru.

"I feel sick," mumbled Nelson, looking pale again as the beetle swayed back and forth.

"I'll eat your lunch for you," Darrel said cheerfully as he took Nelson's lunch and gobbled it up.

Kris sat back to enjoy the ride. His arms and back ached from lifting boxes, but the exercise had felt good, and riding the beetle was fun. It was even more fun because Nelson disliked it so much. The scenery was amazing, with glassy blue rocks and a pale purple sky. Kris thought Droth could be a very cool planet if the people stopped working all the time.

Before long they came to a pile of rocks that was blocking the road. Yolanda carefully steered the beetle through the loose rocks.

"Why don't you have better roads?" Nelson complained.

"We don't have enough people to build them," Yolanda answered harshly.

The beetle suddenly staggered and tipped to the side. Everyone yelled and held on. Yolanda pulled on the levers, but the beetle's legs were stuck. The five kids climbed down to see what had happened, and they saw that the beetle's left front leg was jammed between two boulders.

Yolanda pulled out her phone and called emergency services. She told the boys that the rescue vehicle wouldn't arrive for at least an hour.

"You can't do anything about it," Kris pointed out. "Let's just chill out and relax."

"Idleness is irrational!" Yolanda shouted.

Kris sighed and pulled his **deflated** soccer ball from his pocket. Yoland's eyes widened as the flat ball inflated to its full size.

"It's a self-inflating, carbon-fiber ball," Kris said. "Do you want to play soccer with us?"

Yolanda shook her head, so the boys played and Yolanda watched. After a few minutes, she picked up the ball.

"How do you deflate this thing?" she asked.

STOP AND CHECK

How is Yolanda different from Kris and his friends?

CHAPTER 4
Inflation

"Push all three blue spots **simultaneously**," Kris told her. "That's how you blow it back up, too."

She pushed all three spots at the same time, and the ball deflated. She placed it between two boulders near the trapped beetle leg and then pressed the buttons again.

As the boys watched, the inflating ball pushed at the boulders, forcing them apart. One of the boulders fell to the side, freeing the beetle's leg.

"That was a great idea," Kris told Yolanda.

Yolanda looked pleased but embarrassed. "I got the idea while I was doing nothing, just chilling out as you call it. I don't know how, but it just popped into my head out of nowhere."

"That's the whole point of taking a break," Kris said. "I often get ideas while I'm doing nothing—just playing or staring at the sky."

"He gets great ideas at school," Pedro said with a grin.

"Thanks, Pedro," Kris said, pretending to be insulted. "Anyway, Yolanda, you should take breaks more often."

"Maybe everyone on Droth should take breaks," Yolanda said thoughtfully. "Dad always complains that we can't get workers to move here, and many Drothians move away. We have to work harder every year because we have fewer and fewer workers."

Yolanda called emergency services to cancel the rescue vehicle. Then she called her father.

"I've had a **stupendous** idea," she said. "It's so amazing! It's called a vacation, a special day every year when no one works. It's perfectly logical because taking breaks helps people work more efficiently. It would be something for workers to look forward to each year, an **incentive** to work harder. Maybe it's time for us to broaden our **horizons**. We should also have something called a weekend, which is a whole hour every week for doing nothing."

Kris tried to interrupt and tell her she was getting it wrong. She just glared at him.

Kris smiled and let it go. Maybe Vacation Day and Weekend Hour were exactly what Droth needed.

STOP AND CHECK

Why does life in Droth get harder every year?

Respond to Reading

Summarize

Use details from *Chill Out* to help you summarize the selection. Your graphic organizer may help you.

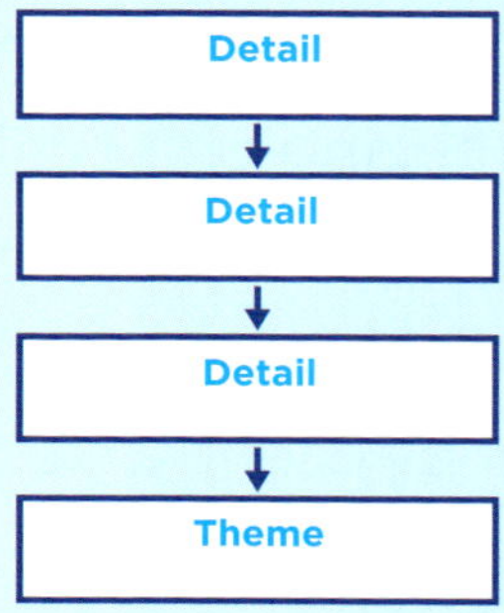

Text Evidence

1. What does Yolanda's experience with the soccer ball teach her? **THEME**

2. Find the word *idleness* on page 9. What clues help you to figure out the word's meaning? **VOCABULARY**

3. Reread pages 15. Write about how Yolanda's dialogue shows the story's main message. Use details from the text. **WRITE ABOUT READING**

Genre Poetry

Compare Texts

Read an ode about Vacation Day on Droth.

Ode to Vacation Day

Today's Droth's first Vacation Day.
No work or school—we snoozed; we played.
We danced, we wrote some poetry.
(That's what I did, as you can see.)
Please don't laugh or slam the door,
I never wrote a rhyme before.
I'm new to creativity,
Imagination roaming free,
A trillion billion thoughts now fall
Into my pen, then bounce and crawl
Around the page until I find
A rhyme that somehow fills my mind.

Today's Droth's first Vacation Day.
"Irrational," my dad did say,
But even he must now admit
That all of Droth does benefit—
This "wasteful" inactivity
Increased our productivity.
Dad's worried what his friends might think
If they, like me, had seen him slink
Outside to sniff the spiral blooms
While humming old romantic tunes.

Today's Droth's first Vacation Day.
Dad and I sat by the bay
In silence, till he turned to me.
"We live on Droth, not Earth, you see.
This planet's harsh, and we are few.
If we don't work hard, then who—"
"I know," I interrupted. "Still,
We sometimes need to sit and chill.
Relaxing is so magical,
So wonderfully illogical,
And that's what makes it so much fun
On Earth or Droth, for anyone."

Make Connections

Why would Yolanda write "Ode to Vacation Day"? **ESSENTIAL QUESTION**

Which key ideas in *Chill Out* are also in "Ode to Vacation Day"? **TEXT TO TEXT**

Focus on Literary Elements

Imagery Imagery is rich, descriptive language. A poet uses imagery to paint a picture in the reader's mind. Imagery can come from words and phrases that appeal to the senses. The poet can also use figurative language, such as metaphors, personification, and hyperbole.

Read and Find In "Ode to Vacation Day," the writer uses sensory descriptions. For example, the speaker sees her dad "slink outside to sniff the spiral blooms." The speaker also uses figurative language when she says "thoughts ... fall into my pen, then bounce and crawl around the page."

Your Turn

Reread *Chill Out*. Look for descriptive details that help you picture what something looks like or how a character speaks or acts. What vivid adjectives help you see the scenery on Droth? What verbs show how the people on Droth move? What adverbs help you hear how Yolanda sounds when she speaks? Where does the author use figurative language to compare two things? Share the words and phrases you found with a partner.